Don't be impatient;
beauty in the garden like
everything else worth having,
is worth waiting for.

DON'TS
FOR
GARDENERS

Copper Beech Publishing

Published in Great Britain by
Copper Beech Publishing Ltd
© Copper Beech Publishing Ltd 2007

ISBN 978 1 898617 42 6

A CIP catalogue record for this book is available
from The British Library.

Copper Beech Gift Books
Copper Beech Publishing Ltd
P O Box 159 East Grinstead
Sussex England RH19 4FS

This pocket sized volume, full of
witty and useful advice in a series
of maxims, is imparted in the
form of Don'ts.
This dainty little book should make
a charming present for any lover
of the natural unaffected
English garden.

"Failures but carve a pathway to
success"
Alfred Austin

"Oh, Tiger-Lily," said Alice
… "I *wish* you could talk."
Tiger-Lily; "when there's anybody
worth talking to."
Alice through the looking-glass.

DON'T fail for want of taking trouble. The gardener who said of some sweet peas that they were "only grown, not cultivated," voiced a subtle distinction.

DON'T be impatient; beauty in the garden – like everything else worth having – is worth waiting for. "With time and patience the leaf of the mulberry tree becomes satin."

DON'T snub the beginner – did *you* never mistake a weed for a flower or put a bulb in upside down?

DON'T grudge work and forethought – let your eye enjoy the present, while your brain is working for the future. "Drudgery is the grey angel of success."

DON'T when your hostess is showing you with pride some fine specimens of roses in her garden, remark – "Yes, it certainly is a wonderful year – *everyone* has good roses!"

DON'T give advice – those who ask it only want to be confirmed in their own opinion!

DON'T be pessimistic!
One real "good to live" day should
balance the evils of many
hours of gloom.

DON'T continue a hoary old habit for no better reason than because such and such a thing *"has always been done."* Like the stud groom who refused to make use of a bathroom because his father had always washed in a stable pail!

DON'T always follow, but lead when the spirit moves you, even if it *does* sometimes land you in a blind alley!

DON'T fill up the interstices
between your old paving stones
with cement, but make the little
spaces into happy homes for
tiny treasures.

DON'T buy a rose because you admire it in a box at a show. It is, perhaps, so top-heavy that, in a garden, it would hang its head and refuse to look you in the face!

DON'T because you (or your gardener for you) can grow flowers or fruit to perfection, think that you necessarily possess everything that a garden *may* mean to one who loves it.

Fig. 5. COLOUR HARMONIES, AND DISCORDS.

The above diagram is intended to show at a glance the relations of the various colours to each other. Thus, take violet (No. I.) we find it harmonises with No. IX. (golden yellow), but clashes with 5—13 (emerald green and red).

DON'T be afraid of trying new ideas, different groupings and colour effects – the possibilities are inexhaustible and the planning a joy, although the exact result you hoped for does not always come off.

DON'T neglect your old garden friends for the new ones. As with the human kind, the old often stand the stress and strain of bad times and bad weather better than the new.

DON'T make your herbaceous borders too narrow – your plans will grow, and over-crowding is fatal to beauty.

DON'T when arranging arches in your garden, be too stereotyped in your choice of material. Try, for instance, laburnum which will make a lovely canopy of gold over your path in the spring.

DON'T be cross if, when just in the middle of a day's gardening – grubby but happy – visitors arrive and all your best laid plans go wrong!

DON'T think of your garden as a place where there *must* be a pergola, a herbaceous border, a sun-dial, a rose and rock-garden – simply because other people have them!

DON'T find a home in your
woodland spaces for garden
flowers, but only try to increase
the natural beauties of the wild
things you find there.

DON'T mourn the disappearance of the flowers which have been succeeded by something better; like the old-fashioned verbena and sweet-william (how lovely in their present guise) or the ugly, muddy-coloured petunia of our youth.

DON'T be satisfied with directing only. Dig, delve, and plant, yourself – health and pure enjoyment will follow.

DON'T walk always on the dull plains of fact, but wander sometimes in the flowery paths of fancy!

DON'T be afraid of your emotions. The beauty of a border in the spring, the riot of roses in the summer - the glory of a mass of white lilies seen at night by the light of the moon – who would not be thrilled by the sight of these?

DON'T be too precise. Directly one knows – or thinks one knows – exactly what is going to happen, half the joy is lost, but the un-known may bring poetry and beauty in her train!

DON'T miss a single one of nature's joys – the song of the birds as well as the beauty and scent of the flowers – all are wanted to make nature's scheme complete!

DON'T let the details of the
garden – important though they be
– absorb you too much, but rather
think about the big effects, so
much more satisfying for the
eye and mind.

Fig. 8. HARMONIOUS COLOUR PROGRESSION.
The above diagram shows the proper sequence of colours to produce a harmonious blend. In planting a border, therefore, with hardy perennials, annuals, etc., commence with No. 1 colour, deep blue, and follow on in order until violet (No. 13) is reached, then proceed in the same order if further space has to be planted.

DON'T on the other hand, be afraid of formality in its proper place: - the Dutch garden, with its closely clipped yew hedges, tiled paths and conventional grouping of bulbs and flowers – makes its own special appeal to the garden lover.

DON'T think there is a 'Royal Road' to gardening, though experience and a real love of it will teach you some useful short cuts.

DON'T be 'superior' – even a daisy could teach you something if it could speak!

DON'T make your garden simply a spot where flowers are grown, but let it mean something more: a poem – a picture – or a little bit of fairy-land.

DON'T worry about botanical names, but leave these to the learned professors, who are so busy labelling the different families that they forget to admire their progeny.

DON'T be a flower-*fancier*, fixing your attention on the minute marking of a bulb, or the precise formation of a rose-bud, but leave these things to the scientists, while you join the happy ranks of the flower-*lovers*.

DON'T despair when your plants look a little drooping and dyspeptic, but study their likes and dislikes, and give them food they can digest and assimilate.

DON'T make your garden like a cemetery! Label discreetly, hiding the names of your plants under their foliage.

DON'T hesitate to banish those old derelicts – borders of crude scarlet geraniums, small yellow calceolarias, and dark blue lobelias – sacred to the memory of early Victorian gardeners!

DON'T abuse the English climate too much! Without the damp of which you complain your lawns would not be so green, or your primroses flourish so abundantly.

DON'T forget that nature must have a free hand if she is to work her wonderful way with you, so leave drab duty behind in the house, and take into the garden the joy of living!

DON'T let little jealousies and little meannesses mar the pleasure of your garden, but find time to admire other people's efforts while you struggle with your own!

**DON'T be too proud to learn –
nature is there waiting to speak if
you are ready to listen.**

DON'T enlarge your garden too much; the more it gets beyond your own eye and care, the less real enjoyment you will gain from it.

DON'T have too many irons in the fire. It is better to cultivate a few things well than a lot badly.

DON'T be irritated by people who walk through a garden – seeing nothing – rather be profoundly sorry for them!

DON'T try to control nature too much, or baulk her wondrous ways of using the simplest means for making things of beauty.

DON'T ask to be taken round
a friend's garden, and then –
ignoring the flowers – commence
an animated conversation on
other topics!

DON'T let your gardener stake
and tie your Michaelmas Daisies so
that they look like fat umbrellas
with bands round their waists!
Rather, with a green string above
and below, restrain without
distorting, their graceful growth.

DON'T fret over the darkness of
winter, which has so many beauties
of its own. Are trees ever more
lovely than when their lacy
branches are outlined against
a wintry sky?

DON'T miss the simple joys of life. Most things that are really worth having are within reach of us all, but we must have the eyes to see, and the heart to feel their beauty.

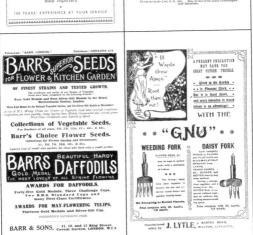

ETIQUETTE FOR COFFEE LOVERS
Fresh coffee – the best welcome in the world! Enjoy the story of coffee drinking, etiquette and recipes.

ETIQUETTE FOR CHOCOLATE LOVERS
Temptation through the years. A special treat for all chocolate lovers.

THE ETIQUETTE OF NAMING THE BABY
'A good name keeps its lustre in the dark.'
Old English Proverb

THE ETIQUETTE OF AN ENGLISH TEA
How to serve a perfect English afternoon tea; traditions, recipes and how to read your fortune in the tea-leaves afterwards.

THE ETIQUETTE OF ENGLISH PUDDINGS
Traditional recipes for good old-fashioned puddings together with etiquette notes for serving.

ETIQUETTE FOR GENTLEMEN
'If you have occasion to use your handkerchief do so as noiselessly as possible.'

RECIPES FOR AN ENGLISH TEA

Recipes for the very best scones, preserves and cakes; recipes for cleaning the silverware - even a recipe for a spotless teapot!

RECIPES FOR HIGH-CLASS COOKERY

Good cooking creates a good impression. Just add a damask cloth, polished glasses and glistening silverware!

RECIPES FOR GARDENERS

Trusted hints and recipes from Victorian days - perfect for any keen gardener.

ETIQUETTE FOR WINE LOVERS

'It is not etiquette to ask a lady to take wine while eating fish or soup.'

For your free catalogue, write to:

**Copper Beech Publishing Ltd
P O Box 159 East Grinstead
Sussex England RH19 4FS
www.copperbeechpublishing.co.uk**

www.copperbeechpublishing.co.uk